SALTOPUS
AND OTHER FIRST DINOSAURS

by Dougal Dixon

illustrated by
Steve Weston and James Field

PICTURE WINDOW BOOKS
Minneapolis, Minnesota

Picture Window Books
5115 Excelsior Boulevard
Suite 232
Minneapolis, MN 55416
877-845-8392
www.picturewindowbooks.com

Printed in the United States of America.

Library of Congress Cataloging-in-Publication Data
Dixon, Dougal.
Saltopus and other first dinosaurs / by Dougal
Dixon ; illustrated by Steve Weston & James Field.
p. cm. – (Dinosaur find)
Includes bibliographical references and index.
ISBN 1-4048-1328-4
1. Dinosaurs—Juvenile literature. I. Weston, Steve, ill.
II. Field, James, 1959- ill. III. Title.
QE861.5.D647 2006
567.9—dc22   2005023335

Acknowledgments
This book was produced for Picture Window Books by
Bender Richardson White, U.K.

Illustrations by James Field (pages 4–5, 9, 11, 13, 19)
and Steve Weston (cover and pages 7,
15, 17, 19, 21).
Diagrams by Stefan Chabluk.
All photographs copyright Digital Vision.

Consultant: John Stidworthy, Scientific Fellow of
the Zoological Society, London, and former
Lecturer in the Education Department, Natural
History Museum, London.

Reading Adviser: Susan Kesselring, M.A., Literacy
Educator, Rosemount-Apple Valley-Eagan
(Minnesota) School District

Types of dinosaurs
In this book, a red shape at the
top of a left-hand page shows
the animal was a meat-eater.
A green shape shows it was
a plant-eater.

**Just how big—or small—
were they?**
Dinosaurs were many different
sizes. We have compared their
sizes to one of the following:

Chicken
2 feet (60 centimeters) tall
6 pounds (2.7 kilograms)

Adult person
6 feet (1.8 meters) tall
170 pounds (76.5 kg)

Elephant
10 feet (3 m) tall
12,000 pounds
(5,400 kg)

TABLE OF CONTENTS

WHAT'S INSIDE?

Dinosaurs lived between 230 and 65 million years ago. These dinosaurs were some of the first. Find out how they lived and what they have in common with today's animals.

THE FIRST DINOSAURS

The first dinosaurs were mostly small. Among the early dinosaurs were fierce meat-eaters, two-footed plant-eaters, and long-necked plant-eaters. These dinosaurs lived in all parts of the world about 230 million years ago when the climate was hot and dry.

Saturnalia, a long-necked plant-eater, and *Abrictosaurus*, a two-footed plant-eater, fed on the plants of the desert. They had to watch out for meat-eating dinosaurs that wanted to eat them, like *Staurikosaurus*.

SALTOPUS

Pronunciation:
SAWL-tuh-PUSS

It was safer for the first dinosaurs to hunt by night. In those times, there were fierce animals like big crocodiles that hunted by day. At night, *Saltopus* hunted for food that the other meat-eaters would not find.

Nightime hunters today

Like *Saltopus* did millions of years ago, lions often hunt at sunset.

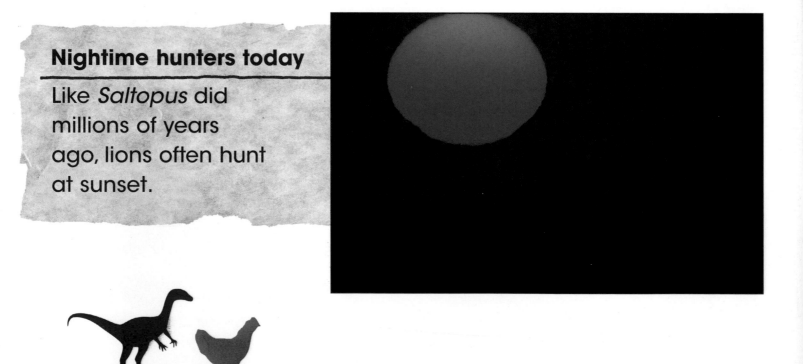

Size Comparison

Saltopus was a little animal with long legs that were good for running. It caught insects as it ran through forests at night.

SATURNALIA

Pronunciation:
SAT-ur-NAIL-ee-uh

Saturnalia walked on four legs and had a long neck. It used its neck to reach around for the kinds of plants that it liked to eat. The colored pattern of its skin helped it hide among rocks.

Rock hiders today

The Galapagos land iguana eats tough plants growing between rocks like *Saturnalia* did.

Size Comparison

10

Saturnalia lived in the few damp places in the deserts. There were enough plants there for it to survive.

Plateosaurus was one of the first plant-eating dinosaurs. It could eat plants on the ground or leaves high in trees. It used its big thumb claws to pull down branches. *Plateosaurus* lived mostly in herds.

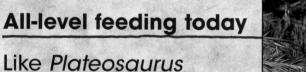

All-level feeding today

Like *Plateosaurus* once did, elephants eat food on the ground, in bushes, and high in trees.

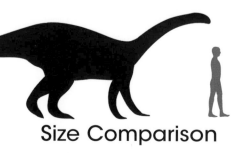

Size Comparison

Plateosaurus ate mostly ferns. It also ate the leaves of palm-like trees called cycads and the needle-like leaves of coniferous trees.

LILIENSTERNUS

Some of the early meat-eating dinosaurs were big, strong, sleek, and fast. Among them was *Liliensternus.* It had a bright crest on its head so that other *Liliensternus* would recognize it.

Pack hunters today

Wolves are big, fierce hunters that chase after prey in packs like *Liliensternus* did long ago.

Size Comparison

14

Liliensternus prowled along the river banks in packs. They looked for animals that had come to drink. Sometimes they attacked plant-eating animals that were stuck in the river mud.

MELANOROSAURUS

Pronunciation:
muh-LAN-oh-ruh-SAW-rus

Melanorosaurus had a small head, long neck, long tail, thick body, and short legs. It lived in herds so that the meat-eaters would think twice about attacking it.

Long necks today

Giraffes have long necks and feed from the tops of trees like *Melanorosaurus* did millions of years ago.

Size Comparison

Melanorosaurus was one of the earliest large plant-eaters. With its long neck, it reached up to the juiciest leaves at the tops of trees.

ABRICTOSAURUS

Pronunciation:
ab-RICK-tuh-SAW-rus

Abrictosaurus was one of the first two-footed plant-eating dinosaurs. It ran across the dusty plains looking for all kinds of food. It had some teeth for ripping plants from the ground and others for chewing food.

Diggers today

Squirrels dig food from the ground and have different types of teeth like *Abrictosaurus*.

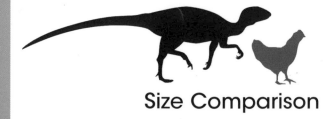

Size Comparison

18

Abrictosaurus had big hands. It used them for digging and scraping away earth around plants. That way it could reach the roots and underground shoots that it liked to eat.

COELOPHYSIS

Pronunciation:
SEE-lo-FY-sis

Coelophysis hunted in packs. It chased animals and killed them. Sometimes it ate animals that had already been killed. When there was no other food, it killed and ate other *Coelophysis*.

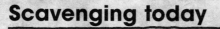

Scavenging today

Like *Coelophysis* once did, lions often eat prey that other animals have killed. They chase away other meat-eaters.

Size Comparison

20

If a *Coelophysis* was really hungry, it would fight with others in the pack to be the first to eat.

WHERE DID THEY GO?

Dinosaurs are extinct, which means that none of them are alive today. Scientists study rocks and fossils to find clues about what happened to dinosaurs.

People have different explanations about what happened. Some people think a huge asteroid hit Earth and caused all sorts of climate changes, which caused the dinosaurs to die. Others think volcanic eruptions caused the climate to change and that killed the dinosaurs. No one knows for sure what happened to all the dinosaurs.

GLOSSARY

claws—tough, usually curved fingernails or toenails

climate—the general weather conditions

coniferous—an evergreen tree that has cones

crest—structure on top of the head or back, usually used to signal to other animals

cycads—plants like conifers but with a thick trunk and palm-like leaves

herds—large groups of animals that move, feed, and sleep together

insects—small, six-legged animals; they include ants, bees, beetles, and flies

packs—groups of animals that hunt and kill together

plains—large areas of flat land with few large plants

prey—animals that are hunted by other animals for food

scavenging—taking and eating prey killed by other animals

To Learn More

At the Library

Clark, Neil, and William Lindsay. *1001 Facts About Dinosaurs.* New York: Backpack Books, Dorling Kindersley, 2002.

Dixon, Dougal. *Dougal Dixon's Amazing Dinosaurs.* Honesdale, Penn.: Boyds Mills Press, 2000.

Holtz, Thomas, and Michael Brett-Surman. *Jurassic Park Institute Dinosaur Field Guide.* New York: Random House, 2001.

On the Web

FactHound offers a safe, fun way to find Web sites related to this book. All of the sites on FactHound have been researched by our staff.

1. Visit *www.facthound.com*
2. Type in this special code: 1404813284
3. Click on the FETCH IT button.

Your trusty FactHound will fetch the best sites for you!

Look for all of the books in the Dinosaur Find series:

Index